W9-ANT-564

Renewable Energy

Edited by Aaron Carr

www.av2books.com

AV² provides enriched content that supplements and complements this book. Weigl's AV² books strive to create inspired learning and engage young minds in a total learning experience.

Your AV² Media Enhanced books come alive with...

Audio
Listen to sections of the book read aloud.

Key Words
Study vocabulary, and complete a matching word activity.

Video
Watch informative video clips.

Quizzes
Test your knowledge.

Embedded Weblinks
Gain additional information for research.

Slide Show
View images and captions, and prepare a presentation.

Try This!
Complete activities and hands-on experiments.

... and much, much more!

Go to www.av2books.com, and enter this book's unique code.

BOOK CODE

Q424374

AV² by Weigl brings you media enhanced books that support active learning.

Download the AV² catalog at www.av2books.com/catalog

AV² Online Navigation on page 48

Published by AV² by Weigl
350 5th Avenue, 59th Floor
New York, NY 10118

Websites: www.av2books.com   www.weigl.com

Copyright ©2015 AV² by Weigl
All rights reserved. No part of this publication may be reproduced, stored in a retrieval system, or transmitted in any form or by any means, electronic, mechanical, photocopying, recording, or otherwise, without the prior written permission of the publisher.

Library of Congress Control Number: 2014940096

ISBN 978-1-4896-1110-9 (hardcover)
ISBN 978-1-4896-1111-6 (softcover)
ISBN 978-1-4896-1112-3 (single-user eBook)
ISBN 978-1-4896-1113-0 (multi-user eBook)

Printed in the United States of America in North Mankato, Minnesota
1 2 3 4 5 6 7 8 9 0 18 17 16 15 14

052014
WEP090514

Weigl acknowledges Getty Images as its primary image supplier for this title.

Every reasonable effort has been made to trace ownership and to obtain permission to reprint copyright material. The publishers would be pleased to have any errors or omissions brought to their attention so that they may be corrected in subsequent printings.

Project Coordinator: Aaron Carr
Art Director: Terry Paulhus

Renewable Energy

CONTENTS

Introduction to Renewable Energy

What would happen if we had no more fuel to heat homes, operate factories, drive cars, and produce electricity? It is not as farfetched as it sounds. Earth is running out of fossil fuels. Fossil fuels, which include oil, coal, and natural gas, power almost everything in the modern world. They contain carbon and are formed from the remains of prehistoric plants and animals. They also exist in limited amounts. An alternative to fossil fuels is called renewable energy. This kind of energy comes from natural resources available in unlimited quantities. Examples include water, wind, and sunlight.

Hydropower

"Rushing water can supply a factory with energy. It can power a light bulb and keep a building cool in the summer."

Wind Power

"Currently, more than 3 percent of all the electricity produced in the United States comes from wind power."

Solar Energy

Other Forms of Renewable Energy

"The Sun generates more energy every second than all the power plants on Earth could produce in 2 million years."

"One way to reduce the need for fossil fuels is to create energy from plants such as corn, wheat, soybeans, and sunflowers."

Hydropower

KEY CONCEPTS

1 The Power of Water

2 Global Warming

3 Greenhouse Gases

4 Kilowatts, Megawatts, and Gigawatts

5 Turbines and Generators

Oil and coal are the world's main fossil fuels. The United States consumes 18.55 million barrels of oil a day. A barrel of oil is equal to 42 gallons (160 liters). The world uses more than 87.4 million barrels per day. Experts say, at this rate, Earth will run out of oil in about 40 years. Supplies of coal will be used up in about 75 to 200 years. Other sources of power will be needed.

1 The Power of Water

One type of renewable energy is hydroelectric power. It is also called hydropower. This is electricity generated from rushing water.

Humans around the world have been using the power of water for centuries. Thousands of years ago, the Greeks had to pound wheat into flour by hand. Then, a machine that captured the power of running water was invented. It was known as the waterwheel. People began using water power to grind wheat. Water power also ran mills that sawed logs into lumber.

Today, dams on rivers use a version of the ancient waterwheel to produce electricity. About 20 percent of the world's electricity comes from hydropower. The largest hydroelectric plant is the Three Gorges Dam in China. This dam uses 32 waterwheels called **turbines**.

However, large dams can cause problems. When a dam blocks the flow of a major river, it can damage plants, animals, and people. Sometimes, governments or companies make the decision that the benefits of the dam outweigh damage to the environment.

The Three Gorges Dam stretches 1.4 miles (2.3 kilometers) across the Yangtze River.

2 Global Warming

Global warming is the gradual increase of Earth's average temperature. In the opinion of many scientists, human activities that burn fossil fuels contribute to global warming. Those activities include driving cars that run on gasoline and burning coal to produce electricity. The burning of fossil fuels releases substances such as **carbon dioxide** into the atmosphere, the layer of gases that surround Earth. Carbon dioxide helps the atmosphere to hold in heat.

The planet's temperature has increased about 1° Fahrenheit (0.55° Celsius) during the past century. Earth's coldest regions have warmed significantly more. Many plant and animal **species** are at risk of dying out in their natural ranges because of this increase in temperature.

Scientists working with the National Aeronautics and Space Administration (NASA) predict that Earth's temperature will rise between 4° and 10°F (2° and 6°C) by the end of the 21st century. In fact, global temperatures are rising faster than at any other time in the past 1,000 years. Reducing the world's carbon dioxide **emissions** in the future may help prevent global warming. Producing electricity using water power does not add carbon dioxide to the atmosphere.

> "The planet's temperature has increased 1°F (0.55°C) during the past century."

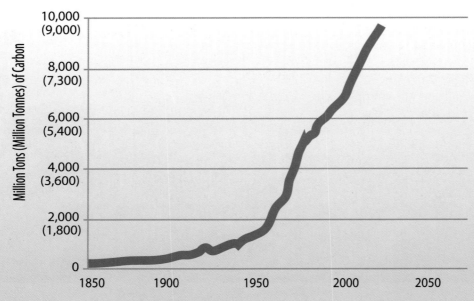

Global Fossil Fuel Emissions, 1850–2012

Million Tons (Million Tonnes) of Carbon

10,000 (9,000)
8,000 (7,300)
6,000 (5,400)
4,000 (3,600)
2,000 (1,800)
0

1850 1900 1950 2000 2050

Should Governments Move People to Build Hydroelectric Projects?

In the 1990s, China's government officials forced more than 1.3 million people from their homes to build the Three Gorges Dam on the Yangtze River. Most of these people had little opportunity to oppose the project. Supporters of the Three Gorges Dam said it was needed to prevent floods in the area and to decrease China's dependence on fossil fuels. Today, around the world, the building of large-scale hydroelectric projects continues to be a political issue.

Some Government Officials
Communities need the electricity, jobs, tax income, and increased business that a large renewable-energy project can provide. Displacing a few people for the good of the country is not too much to ask.

Project Engineers
Flooding near large rivers is often a problem. Large hydro projects, such as the Three Gorges Dam, provide flood control. This dam has protected many people when severe storms have hit.

Some Community Activists
Hydroelectric projects decrease the use of fossil fuel and help stop the effects of **climate change**. However, governments must balance energy needs against the damage such large-scale projects can have on local areas. We do not support forcing people to move.

Some Homeowners
I live in an area near a proposed dam and have been asked to move to a new location. I do not want to lose my home. Government officials should respect the rights of all residents.

For — Supportive — Undecided — Unsupportive — Against

3 Greenhouse Gases

A greenhouse is a glass structure in which plants grow. The glass traps heat inside, keeping the building warm. Earth's atmosphere does the same thing with heat from the Sun. The atmosphere contains greenhouse gases. The more greenhouse gases there are in the atmosphere, the hotter Earth becomes.

This is called the greenhouse effect. Plants, soil, and surface water absorb some of the Sun's energy that reaches Earth, while the planet's surface reflects some back into outer space. However, greenhouse gases in the atmosphere keep some of the Sun's heat close to the surface.

If there were no greenhouse effect, Earth would be frozen rock. Some greenhouse gases, such as carbon dioxide and **methane**, occur naturally. However, humans add more greenhouse gases into the atmosphere by burning fossil fuels and using chlorofluorocarbons. Chlorofluorocarbons (CFCs) are gases once commonly used in cleaning products and aerosol sprays. Since the 1990s, use of CFCs has greatly declined, but they remain in the atmosphere for a long time. Humans added 9.7 billion tons (8.8 billion tonnes) of carbon dioxide into the atmosphere in 2012 alone.

More than 70 percent of Earth's surface is covered with water. Since hydroelectric power does not produce any greenhouse gases, scientists are studying new ways to use ocean tides, waves, and currents to generate electricity. The rise and fall of tides, for example, can drive turbines. The tides fill a storage basin with water. As water enters and leaves the basin, the moving water rotates a turbine.

During cold weather, a greenhouse traps the energy of the Sun and keeps the plants warm.

4 Kilowatts, Megawatts, and Gigawatts

Electricity is measured in watts. One kilowatt, or kW, is equal to 1,000 watts. That is the amount of energy needed to light 10 100-watt light bulbs. One megawatt, or MW, is one million watts, or 1,000 kilowatts. A gigawatt, or GW, is the equivalent of one billion watts, or 1,000 megawatts. A terawatt, or TW, is equal to 1,000 gigawatts.

Hydropower is the world's largest source of renewable energy. It is also the most **efficient** means of producing electricity. A typical fossil fuel plant is able to turn about 50 percent of the stored energy in the fuel into electricity. A large-scale hydropower plant converts about 90 percent of the moving water's energy. Two-thirds of the world's possible hydropower sources remain untapped. Experts estimate that the amount of electricity produced using water power will grow about 3 percent per year over the next few decades.

The United States is the world's fourth-largest producer of hydroelectric power, after China, Brazil, and Canada.

Building hydropower plants can be very expensive. Once a plant is built, however, the cost of producing electricity is much lower than generating electricity by burning fossil fuels.

Not all hydropower systems have the same capacity. The Three Gorges Dam is able to generate 22,500 megawatts of hydroelectricity. Micro-hydropower plants produce less than 100 kilowatts. Mini-hydropower plants can produce between 100 kilowatts and 1 megawatt. Facilities that produce between 1 and 10 megawatts are known as "small." One megawatt provides enough electricity to power about 1,000 households. Small facilities are not able to power a major city, but they are ideal for smaller communities.

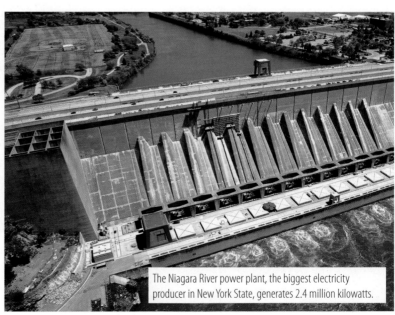

The Niagara River power plant, the biggest electricity producer in New York State, generates 2.4 million kilowatts.

5 Turbines and Generators

At the heart of all hydroelectric plants are their turbines. When rushing water forces a turbine to spin, a shaft attached to the turbine also rotates. This shaft is connected to a generator.

The generator then uses the spinning of the turbine to produce electricity. A generator is a machine that changes mechanical energy into electric energy, or electricity. As long as the turbine spins, the generator produces electricity.

Engineers are working to improve the design of turbines to reduce friction. This is a force that slows down the motion of something that is touching something else. If friction is reduced, a turbine can help turn more of the water's movement into electricity.

People tend to use less electricity at night or on weekends. During these times, the generated hydroelectricity can be sent to batteries. This stored energy can be used later. During times of lower demand for electricity, power produced at a hydroelectric plant can also be used for other things. For example, this power can reverse turbines and pump water up into a **reservoir**. When demand becomes high again, engineers can release the water, which falls onto and spins the turbines.

Turbines spin inside hydroelectric generators at the Hoover Dam in Boulder City, Nevada. The facility generates more than 4 billion kilowatt-hours of hydroelectric power each year for use in Nevada, Arizona, and California.

Should People Be Concerned about the Environmental Costs of Dams?

Hydroelectric power is not expensive to produce. However, many people do not support the construction of more small hydroelectric projects. They are concerned that small, low-power dams will upset the flow and quality of water. The dams block important nutrients, sand, and stones from flowing downstream. The dams also slow the movement of fish and other animal species.

Local Fisher Groups
Hydroelectric projects can destroy an **ecosystem**. They can kill off the local fish population. Harming the environment in these ways can damage the ability of people in the fishing industry to earn a living. That is just as important as the other jobs this project would create.

Some Concerned Parents
I understand that the country needs alternatives to fossil fuels. However, I worry that a dam might affect our environment. I would like to learn more about possible costs to my community.

Local Business Associations
Our community needs the valuable jobs in engineering, construction, and plant operation that this kind of project offers. Many small businesses in the area would benefit from having a power company hiring in the community. However, we support protecting our community's animals and forests.

Power Company Executives
We owe it to our shareholders, the people who invest in our company, to do everything we can to become profitable. We owe it to our customers to provide the cheapest source of available power. As long as we follow the local, state, and federal environmental laws, there is no reason to delay any hydro project.

| For | Supportive | Undecided | Unsupportive | Against |

Wind Power

KEY CONCEPTS

J ust as they used hydropower for centuries, humans have used the power of the wind. Sailors caught the blowing breezes in their ship's sails to travel across vast oceans. People in Europe and the Middle East used windmills to grind grain into flour. However, the idea of generating electricity from wind is new.

1 Benefits and Costs

Many people call Roscoe, Texas, "Wind City, U.S.A." That is because it is home to the country's largest **wind farm**. This farm has 627 wind turbines. These devices capture the energy of moving air, or wind, to produce electricity. Unlike burning fossil fuels, generating electricity using wind energy does not add **pollution** or greenhouse gases to the environment. The Roscoe Wind Farm can produce enough electricity to power 265,000 homes.

The United States is second only to China in wind-power generation. In 2013, the United States produced around 60,000 megawatts of electricity from wind. China generated about 91,000 megawatts.

Currently, more than 3 percent of all the electricity produced in the United States comes from wind power.

Wind is rarely in short supply. However, it blows more in some places than in others. For example, the Roscoe Wind Farm sits on flat land where nothing blocks the breeze. Other turbines are located on hills and offshore.

Operating wind farms costs society in different ways. Spinning wind turbines have been called noisy. Some communities believe the tall structures spoil the beauty of natural areas. Wind farms take natural habitat from various types of wildlife. Turbines also harm or kill birds that fly into their blades.

According to the U.S. Department of Energy, at a distance of 750 to 1,000 feet (230 to 300 meters), a modern wind farm produces about as much noise as a home refrigerator.

Mapping Renewable Energy

North America

Pacific Ocean

Atlantic Ocean

In 2011, countries with some of the world's largest economies produced varying portions of the total electricity they generated from the renewable sources wind, solar, **geothermal**, tidal, and wave power.

South America

Legend

- ☐ Greater than 15 percent
- ☐ 5 percent or above
- ■ Less than 5 percent

Arctic Ocean

Europe

Asia

Africa

Indian Ocean

Pacific Ocean

Australia

Southern Ocean

N
W   E
S

SCALE

1,200 Miles

1,200 Kilometers

2 Oil Crisis

There continues to be interest in expanding the use of wind and other forms of renewable energy. Fossil fuels pollute the air, contribute to global warming, and are in limited supply. In addition, people have to rely on the countries that can supply fossil fuels, especially oil.

In 1973, a conflict in the Middle East called the Yom Kippur War took place. The Arab countries of Egypt and Syria attacked the Jewish state of Israel. The United States supported Israel with weapons and equipment. This angered members of the Organization of the Petroleum Exporting Countries (OPEC), including Iran, Kuwait, and Saudi Arabia. The organization began a series of oil price increases and placed an embargo, or ban, on oil shipments to the United States. The result was a price increase of nearly 200 percent.

These events led to severe shortages of gasoline and heating oil in the United States. Lines at gas stations were common across the country. U.S. president Richard Nixon reduced the national highway speed limit to conserve fuel. The oil crisis contributed to a major economic downturn. It forced many Americans to think about alternative sources of power, such as hydro, solar, and wind energy. By 1974, the oil-producing countries had lifted the embargo against the United States. Still, the need for oil remained.

During the 1970s, gasoline stations in the United States often ran out of fuel.

3 Wind Farms

The uneven heating of Earth's surface by the Sun causes the wind to blow. As Earth warms, so does the atmosphere. Warm air rises and cooler air moves in to take its place. This makes the air move.

Wind farms often consist of rows of towers that are about 165 to 300 feet (50 to 90 m) high. The top of each tower, or turbine, usually looks like a huge fan. Wind hitting the blades causes them to spin. The spinning blades turn a shaft connected to a generator that produces electricity. The electricity can be stored in batteries to be used when the wind dies down.

Turbines are designed and placed to capture as much wind energy as possible. For example, wind travels more slowly at ground level because of friction with the ground. That is why turbine towers are tall. The wind often blows faster along the coast and over large bodies of water. It also blows faster on open ground, such as the Great Plains in the United States.

Wind-Power Production Capacity by Country

Each country's total capacity to produce electricity from wind energy is measured in megawatts. The 2013 world total was 318,105 megawatts.

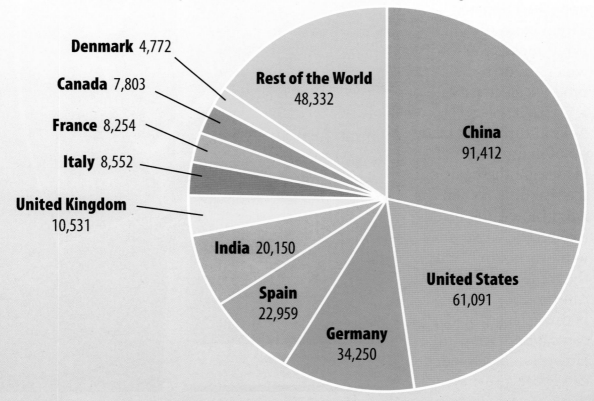

Denmark 4,772
Canada 7,803
France 8,254
Italy 8,552
United Kingdom 10,531
Rest of the World 48,332
China 91,412
India 20,150
Spain 22,959
Germany 34,250
United States 61,091

4 Operating and Furling

Wind turbines come in many designs. Some look like eggbeaters. Others have blades shaped like the wings of an airplane. Small wind turbines, used for homes, produce up to 100 kilowatts of electricity. Larger wind turbines can generate several megawatts.

It is possible to think of a wind turbine as a fan that works backwards. Electricity turns the rotors. They are the parts of the machine that rotate. The revolving rotors produce wind. The opposite happens with a wind turbine. Wind moves the rotors, which, in turn, helps produce electricity.

A wind turbine is made up of many parts. The blades are the heart of the machine. When the wind blows, the blades rotate. The larger a wind turbine's blades, the more electricity it can produce. That is because larger blades can catch more wind. However, large blades can cause a turbine to overheat when they catch too much wind and spin too fast. Strong winds can also damage large blades. To prevent this, a wind turbine is designed to change the angle of its blades or stop the rotors from moving during a high-wind event, such as a storm. This process is called furling.

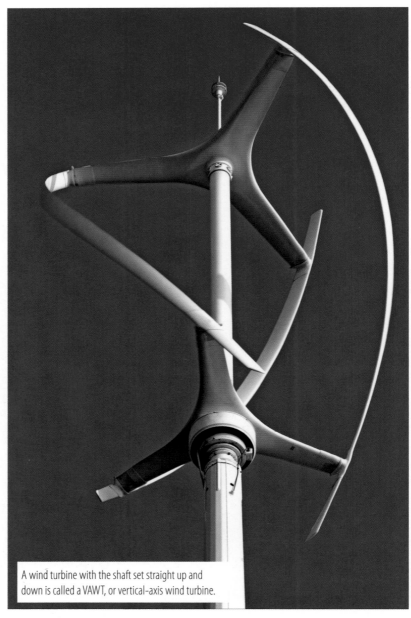

A wind turbine with the shaft set straight up and down is called a VAWT, or vertical-axis wind turbine.

Should There Be Regulations to Protect Birds from Turbines?

In 2012, wind farms killed about 573,000 birds in the United States. A 2013 study found that U.S. wind farms had killed at least 67 federally protected bald and golden eagles since 2008. Birds fly into turbine blades, towers, and power lines. Tree bat populations, which seem to be attracted to the tall turbines, have also been damaged by the growth in wind farms.

Animal Rights Organizations
The U.S. government must balance renewable energy with conservation. It must not sacrifice any species just to produce more energy. This includes our national bird, the bald eagle.

Bird Watchers
Reducing any regulations that protect animal life encourages industries to continue to damage our natural world without penalty. We are concerned about how much we spend on electricity. However, we do not support the killing of birds for lower energy costs.

Government Officials
Wind farms are not a large danger to birds, including protected species. Communication towers, which kill up to 5 million birds a year, and cats, which kill hundreds of millions of birds annually, are far greater threats.

Energy Companies
Any regulations can be costly for our shareholders, our employees, and our customers. Fines for killing birds have cost millions of dollars. Legal fees can also be expensive. Easing regulations helps us to succeed in this industry and offer more affordable electricity to all of our customers.

For	Supportive	Undecided	Unsupportive	Against

5 Pitch and Yawing

Wind can be unreliable. It does not always blow at the same speed or in the same direction. Adjusting the pitch, or angle, of the blades to face into the wind is vital. So-called pitch controls help maintain the best blade angle. Turning the blades to match changes in the direction of the wind is called yawing. On a wind turbine with pitch control, a device called an electronic controller checks the power production level several times a second. If the wind drops, the device turns the blades back into the wind.

Over the years, engineers and scientists have developed more efficient wind turbines. This has reduced the price of wind energy. In 1981, the typical wind turbine produced 50 kilowatts of power. Today, the largest wind turbines are generating as much as 8 megawatts.

As a result of these improvements, the cost of generating electricity using the power of the wind has decreased dramatically. In 1980, it cost more than 55 cents to generate a kilowatt-hour of electricity. Today, the price is just 6 cents.

A child's pinwheel, like a turbine, must be turned in the right direction to spin as fast as it can in the wind.

Should Governments Pay Part of the Cost to Build Wind Farms?

Experts say wind power could supply more than 20 percent of U.S. electricity needs by 2030. However, the cost of locating the proper site, building a wind farm, and operating it can be large. Some groups support government **subsidies** to construct wind farms. Others argue that tax money should not be spent supporting one industry over another.

Renewable Energy Activists
Our goal is to reduce dependence on fossil fuels. Wind is an important renewable energy. Companies require funding from the government to make wind power a reality.

Department of Energy Officials
We have to support these projects across the country in order to reduce our dependence on fossil fuels and greenhouse gas emissions. While we will not be able to satisfy every group, we should encourage renewable energy growth. The benefits will be worth the costs.

Some Environmental Organizations
We support the development of renewable energy. However, we are concerned about the effect of wind farms on the environment. They take away natural areas that are used by animal life.

Some Taxpayers
I do not want to see my tax dollars spent on government subsidies for wind farms. Utility companies report large profits each year. They should pay the construction costs themselves.

| For | Supportive | Undecided | Unsupportive | Against |

Solar Energy

When it comes to renewable energy, the Sun outshines every other source. The Sun's energy powers cars, homes, even space ships. Solar power is most popular in areas where sunlight is plentiful.

1 Solar Technology

Humans have been using the Sun's energy for centuries. In the 1880s, a solar-powered steam engine ran a printing press in France. Then, humans started using oil as a source of energy. It was abundant and inexpensive. The energy crisis of the 1970s brought a renewed interest in solar power from different groups. They recognized that the Sun was a plentiful, if not necessarily efficient, source of energy.

At the time, engineers explored ways to use the Sun's energy. They figured out how to use solar **radiation**. This energy from the Sun could both warm and cool buildings.

The use of solar power fits into three categories. They are passive solar energy, solar thermal, and photovoltaic. Each system makes use of sunlight in a different way.

Passive solar energy systems use the natural principles of heat transfer instead of using equipment such as furnaces. In passive solar technology systems, a building's walls, windows, and floors often collect and store the Sun's radiation and then release heat.

Solar thermal systems work on a large scale and in certain locations. This kind of system uses mirrors to reflect and concentrate sunlight. The resulting large amount of heat energy can be used to produce electricity. Solar thermal works best in areas that receive a great deal of sunlight.

Photovoltaic, or PV, systems convert the Sun's energy directly into electricity. *Photo* means "light," and *voltaic* means "electric." PV systems are often used in places where power generation is expensive, unreliable, or simply absent.

One example of passive solar heating is large windows on the south side of a house that allow winter sunlight to warm a room.

Areas of the United States receive different amounts of solar radiation that can be used to produce electricity. The Southwest is one of the best areas in the United States for solar radiation.

2 The Sun

What makes the Sun such an enormous source of renewable energy? The Sun generates more energy every second than all the power plants on Earth could produce in 2 million years. Scientists say the Sun's power is equal to 380,000,000,000,000,000,000,000, or 380 quintillion, megawatts.

Why is the Sun so powerful? The Sun is a large ball of super-heated gas. Scientists believe the temperature of the Sun's core is 27 million °F (15 million °C). The Sun gets its enormous energy through a nuclear reaction called fusion.

In fusion, **atoms** of **elements** such as hydrogen combine to create a huge amount of energy. This reaction takes place deep inside the Sun at extremely high temperatures. Fusion converts hydrogen to **helium**. This releases so much energy that the Sun glows.

"The Sun generates more energy every second than all the power plants on Earth could produce in 2 million years."

The Sun is about 93 million miles (150 million km) away. Only a small fraction of its energy reaches Earth. Today, solar-power technology is able to convert only about 10 percent of that energy into usable power.

Will Renewable Energy Help Future Generations?

As nations around the world shift to renewable energy, many people argue a **green** economy will create hundreds of thousands of new jobs. Backed by government **incentives**, many companies are investing in renewable energy. Renewable energy can be produced in the United States. That means the end of unpredictable prices and interruptions to energy supply that sometimes comes with the use of oil from other countries.

Scientists
We must reduce the amount of pollution and greenhouse gases in our environment. Focusing on renewable energy technology will save the planet and stop climate change.

U.S. College Students
The renewable energy sector will offer excellent career opportunities for people with the proper training. Renewable energy will also help the United States invest in protecting the environment and addressing climate change.

Opponents of Government Action
Instead of investing money in renewable energy technologies, the government should be ending regulations that limit the activities of energy companies. We can become energy independent if the government does not interfere with exploration by private companies for new sources of fossil fuels.

Oil Companies
The government should allow us to drill in new areas where we know there are supplies of oil. Renewable energy might be worth more research, but it will never solve all of our energy needs.

| For | Supportive | Undecided | Unsupportive | Against |

3 Photovoltaic Cells

In 1839, the French physicist Alexandre-Edmond Becquerel made an amazing discovery. He noticed that when sunlight falls on certain materials, it generates a small amount of electricity. This discovery meant that humans could produce electricity directly from the Sun.

However, things did not progress as Becquerel and others planned. Early attempts to produce electricity from the Sun's rays were not successful. They succeeded in converting only one percent of incoming light to electricity.

Today's photovoltaic cells turn sunlight directly into electricity much more efficiently. PV cells, also known as solar cells, capture tiny **photons** of light while releasing **electrons**. When these fast-moving electrons are captured, the result is an electric current.

PV cells are made of special materials called **semiconductors**, such as silicon. When light strikes the cell, a certain portion of it is absorbed within the semiconductor material. This allows the energy of the absorbed light to transfer to the semiconductor.

The Sun's energy knocks electrons loose so they can flow freely. By attaching metal contacts to each cell, these electrons can be drawn away. This creates an electric current that will power anything, including light bulbs and washing machines. Connecting many PV cells into an **array** can power a house or factory.

PV cells can convert only 20 to 24 percent of the Sun's power into electricity. Researchers are working to solve this problem. In 2013, scientists at Sharp Corporation set a world record. They succeeded in making a new type of solar cell that converts 44.4 percent of the Sun's energy into electricity.

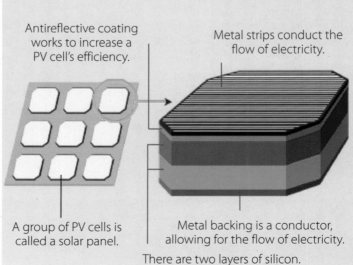

Inside a Photovoltaic Cell

A solar panel captures sunlight, which is converted to electricity using PV cells. These cells power calculators, cars, and houses.

Antireflective coating works to increase a PV cell's efficiency.

Metal strips conduct the flow of electricity.

A group of PV cells is called a solar panel.

Metal backing is a conductor, allowing for the flow of electricity.

There are two layers of silicon.

4 Solar Systems at Work

Most people are eager to save money on their electricity bills. Some homeowners choose to produce their own electricity using solar energy. Most often, these people have large arrays containing PV cells installed on the part of the roof that gets the most sunlight. Sometimes, solar panels are placed on a home's outside walls or in other locations.

Homes producing electricity with solar-energy systems often remain connected to the local electric power lines. If the solar panels do not produce enough electricity to meet the home's needs, then the homeowner pays for electricity from the local utility. Sometimes, the home's solar system produces more electricity than is needed. In some areas, the extra can be sold to the local utility.

Many homes with solar systems get most, if not all, of the electricity they need from the solar panels. However, solar systems are expensive to buy and have installed. The cost of buying and installing enough solar panels to power a house can be more than $25,000. It could take a household 12 years or more to save that much money on its electricity bills. As PV cells become more efficient, fewer solar panels should be needed to power a home. Therefore, the cost of solar-energy systems should go down in the future.

Until then, some people are choosing to lease rather than buy a solar-energy system. That can cost more than $100 each month. However, the homeowner then pays so little each month to the local utility for electricity that he or she is still spending less overall than before the solar system was leased.

Solar panels have also been installed on office towers and other large buildings to provide all or part of a building's electricity needs. Panels containing PV cells have other uses as well. Sometimes, they power emergency telephones alongside highways or lights at highway exit ramps.

Road signs can be powered by the energy of the Sun.

The Ivanpah Solar Electric Generating System features three towers that are 460 feet (140 m) high. They are about 45 miles (72 km) southwest of Las Vegas, Nevada.

5 Concentrating Collectors

The Mojave Desert in California always seems sunny. The Sun shines there 330 to 350 days a year. It is an excellent location to generate solar electricity. In 2014, the world's largest solar thermal project, called the Ivanpah Solar Electric Generating System, began operating here.

While photovoltaic technology converts the Sun's energy directly into electricity, the Ivanpah plant uses concentrating, or focusing, solar collectors. It has 170,000 **parabolic** mirrors that focus sunlight on boilers that sit on top of three towers. The Sun's rays heat the water in the towers to 1,000°F (538°C). That creates steam that then turns turbines to generate electricity.

The Ivanpah plant powers about 140,000 homes in California. It generates 377 megawatts of electricity. That is more than double what was once the world's largest solar thermal plant, in southern Spain. Officials say Ivanpah reduces the amount of carbon dioxide emitted into the atmosphere by 400,000 tons (360,000 tonnes) a year.

The Ivanpah plant sits on 3,500 acres (1,400 hectares) of federal land. Some environmental groups have complained about how the plant has hurt animal species. The threatened desert tortoise, for example, lost its natural habitat. Other groups concerned about climate change have praised the project as an important step toward replacing fossil fuel.

Should the Government Encourage Renewable Energy Use?

Governments often encourage homeowners and companies to use renewable energy or to make their homes and businesses more energy efficient. They do this by offering tax refunds or low-interest loans. Supporters of these programs say incentives give people a reason to help the environment. Others say incentives, especially tax money, should be used for clean-energy research and enforcing environmental laws.

Green Business Owners

The government has to support a green economy. Tax breaks or rebates will help me hire more workers and buy more equipment. In the end, those actions will help the economy and help me offer the lowest costs for my valuable products.

Apartment Building Landlords

Purchasing and installing energy-efficient windows, furnaces, and appliances is expensive. A tax rebate or low-interest loan would encourage me to lower the energy use in my buildings, which is a good outcome for everyone.

Oil Companies

Tax credits and other incentives for renewable energy companies and homeowners may damage our ability to remain profitable. In time, we may have a stake in and make money from renewable energy. Careful progress is what is required.

Tax Groups

The government should not be spending tax dollars on green-energy research. Renewable energy is too costly. To be **sustainable**, these green companies must succeed on their own, just like other businesses.

 For   Supportive   Undecided   Unsupportive   Against

Other Forms of Renewable Energy

KEY CONCEPTS

1 Biofuels

2 Biomass

3 Geothermal Energy

Humans need energy to survive in the modern world. Operating factories, heating and cooling buildings, and traveling from place to place require energy. Global energy use will increase by 36 percent over the next 25 years. This will strain current energy supplies. This is why the development of hydro, solar, and wind power is so important. Other forms of renewable energy include biofuels, biomass, and geothermal energy.

1 Biofuels

One way to reduce the need for products such as gasoline is to create fuel from plants, which can be grown over and over again. Fuels made from plants such as corn, wheat, soybeans, and sunflowers are known as biofuels. Scientists are also altering the **genes** of some plant species. They hope to make biofuel crops grow faster and larger.

There are two main types of biofuels. They are bioalcohol and biodiesel. Bioalcohol is a fuel that forms when **organic materials**, such as corn and sugary plants, break down.

Ethanol is a form of bioalcohol. To make ethanol, engineers use yeast and bacteria to break down the sugars in corn and other plants. Some companies produce ethanol from sugarcane. This is six times less expensive than producing ethanol from corn. Growing sugarcane requires the use of fewer chemicals, including fertilizers and pesticides. However, sugarcane farmers often burn fields, which releases greenhouse gases into the atmosphere.

Biodiesel is a fuel produced by a process in which oils from organic material are combined with alcohol. To create biodiesel, refineries use the oil found in crops such as sunflowers and rapeseed plants. Biofuels burn cleaner than fossil fuels. Burning them causes less pollution. Energy companies often mix biofuels with gasoline.

Biofuel crops have the potential to affect society and the environment in a few ways. Some of these crops can grow on land that cannot grow food. Biofuel crops also absorb carbon dioxide from the atmosphere, reducing the amount of greenhouse gases.

The carbon dioxide emissions from burning fossil fuels can harm humans. Breathing tiny particles of pollution contributes to various health problems, such as asthma, lung cancer, and heart disease. A 2013 study found that "ground-level" pollution created by engines that run on fossil fuels, such as cars, cause 200,000 people each year to die earlier than they otherwise would.

2 Biomass

Biomass is plant material and animal waste that is used as fuel. This material is itself burned, rather than being used to make a liquid fuel. Types of biomass include wood, agricultural crops, the stems and stalks that remain after food crops are harvested, and waste such as cow manure. Biomass is sustainable and less expensive than fuel oil, propane, and natural gas. Modern large-scale biomass systems do not produce as much carbon dioxide as burning fossil fuels.

Sources of U.S. Electricity Produced Using Renewable Energy

In 2013, the United States used renewable energy to produce about 13 percent of the electricity generated.

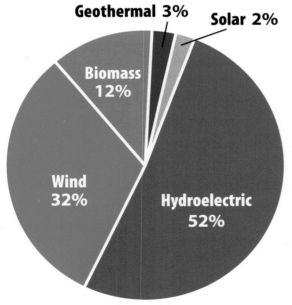

Geothermal 3% Solar 2%

Biomass 12%

Wind 32%

Hydroelectric 52%

Note: Percentages do not add to 100 because of rounding.

3 Geothermal Energy

A huge source of energy, called geothermal energy, comes from below the ground. This energy is drawn from the hot rock and fluid within Earth's crust.

People on the island of Iceland have known about the benefits of geothermal energy for centuries. This nation sits on a crack in Earth's surface where two **tectonic plates** are moving away from each other. The crack allows heat from deep within Earth to move toward the surface. Iceland has huge reservoirs of underground water that are warmed by this heat. Power plants pump the hot water from the ground, allowing the steam to turn turbines that are used to make electricity.

People do not have to live near the boundary of two tectonic plates to benefit from geothermal energy. Just a few feet below the surface, the temperature of underground water remains constant between 42° and 80°F (6° and 27°C), depending on where a person lives. Heat can be pumped up from the ground to warm buildings. The steam that rises from **geysers**, springs, and underground reservoirs can also be used to drive turbines used to create electricity. Wells drilled thousands of feet (m) below Earth's surface recover geothermal energy for commercial use.

Are Food Crops Good Sources of Renewable Energy?

Some people are opposed to making fuel from food crops. They say the crops should be used to feed humans and animals, not generating more energy. Others believe growing fuel crops could be a valuable answer to the current problem of dependence on fossil fuels.

Biofuel Researchers
We are working on turning corn stalks, stems, leaves, and husks as well as wood chips into biofuel without harming the environment. In time, our work will expand our renewable energy resources. It will also lower the cost of producing renewable fuel.

Renewable Energy Trade Associations
Biofuels tend to produce less local pollution than fossil fuels. That is why some countries such as Brazil, which gets 30 percent of its automobile fuel from sugarcane ethanol, has reduced air pollution.

Dairy Farmers
The government gives subsidies to farmers to grow biofuel crops. More land used to grow these crops means less land used to grow crops to feed animals. As a result, the price of animal feed goes up. People will have to pay more for my milk because it costs me more to feed my herd. While I would like more renewable energy options, I do not support the government getting involved in this way.

Social Activists
Producing biofuel often generates more greenhouse gas emissions than gasoline. We are also converting crops that feed people into crops that provide energy. Our actions are damaging, not saving, the planet.

| For | Supportive | Undecided | Unsupportive | Against |

Renewable Energy through History

People have been using renewable energy for centuries. Water, wind, sunlight, and other sources of renewable energy have helped humans do a variety of tasks. As the modern world examines the effects of fossil fuels on climate change, energy that is available in unlimited quantities in nature increases in importance.

5000 BC
Wind energy propels boats along the Nile River in Egypt.

200 BC
Windmills are used to pump water in China and grind grain in Persia and the Middle East.

AD 100
Italian historian Pliny the Younger builds a passive solar home. He uses glass to keep heat in and cold out.

1000s
Windmills are used extensively for food production in the Middle East. Returning merchants and crusaders carry this idea back to Europe.

1300s

1300s
Ancient Pueblo people in North America live in south-facing cliff dwellings that capture the winter Sun.

1767
Swiss scientist Horace de Saussure invents the first solar collector. It was in the form of a solar hot box, a tiny wooden greenhouse with a glass cover.

1767

1962

2009

U.S. president Barack Obama announces a renewable energy goal. He calls for 25 percent of the country's electricity to be generated from renewable sources by 2025.

2009

1800s

U.S. settlers use windmills to pump water for farms and ranches and, later, to generate electricity for homes and industry.

1881

Niagara Falls, New York, lights street lamps using hydropower.

1940

Approximately one-third of electricity generation in the United States comes from hydropower.

1954

Solar cells are invented.

1962

The first geothermal plants in the United States are built at The Geysers in northern California.

1977

The U.S. Department of Energy is established.

1995

The Intergovernmental Panel on Climate Change (IPCC) reports that "the balance of evidence suggests a discernible human influence on global climate."

1997

The Kyoto Conference on Global Climate Change draws international attention to the global warming issue and the connection to fossil fuels.

2008

A plant opens in Wyoming that turns waste wood into ethanol.

2014

The world's largest solar thermal project, the Ivanpah Solar Electric Generating System, opens in California's Mojave Desert.

Renewable Energy Careers

ENGINEER

Duties Design and put into practice new technology for green-energy development

Education A master's or doctorate degree in any of the engineering disciplines

Interest Working on new renewable-energy technologies

There are many types of engineers in the renewable energy field. The most common are mechanical, electrical, and civil engineers, who specialize in structural, water resources, and environment work. Engineers in renewable energy design hydroelectric dams, solar cells, and wind turbines. They work to find new ways to turn plants into energy and use the Sun's energy. Engineers study math, chemistry, and sometimes electricity. An engineer may work for the government, a small company, or a corporation.

ARCHITECT

Duties Design and plan the building of houses and other structures

Education A bachelor's or master's degree

Interest Designing and planning energy-efficient buildings

Architects organize and oversee the development of all types of buildings, including energy-efficient homes, apartment buildings, concert halls, schools, and factories. Developers, home owners, and companies hire architects to create design ideas and then develop these designs. Architects meet regularly with their clients to consult on the styles, features, colors, and materials. They also provide blueprints, or detailed plans, for contractors and construction workers. Architects must ensure that the project stays on schedule and on budget. They earn a university education before being able to practice in the field.

FARMER

Duties Plant and cultivate biomass crops

Education An associate's degree or higher at a college of agriculture

Interest Producing crops that can be turned into biofuels

Farming is a challenging, varied occupation. Many farmers go to school to study business and the science of raising and caring for plants and fruit. Many have on-the-job experience. There is a large need for farmer to grow soybeans, sugarcane, wheat, and switchgrass, crops that can be turned into ethanol or other biofuels. Farmers who are not in the biofuel business can often turn farm waste, such as cornstalks and cow manure, into biofuel.

SOLAR PANEL INSTALLER

Duties Install solar panels on buildings such as schools, homes, and businesses

Education A high school diploma, plus electrical training

Interest Renewable energy and electrical systems

Solar panel installers often work for companies that sell solar panels. These trained workers assemble, install, and maintain photovoltaic systems. Their customers are residents, governments, and businesses. Installers must measure, cut, bolt, and put together the solar panel units. Solar panel installers operate small power tools and often work outdoors.

Key Renewable Energy Organizations

DOE

Goal Use technology and science to ensure the security and prosperity of the United States as it relates to energy use

Reach United States

Facts Has 17 national laboratories for research and development

The U.S. Department of Energy (DOE) often takes the lead role in developing renewable energy resources. Scientists that work for the department's many laboratories have developed various energy technologies. The DOE also provides funding for companies in the energy research and technology field. Through its many offices, the DOE provides education and training programs in the renewable energy field. With the Environmental Protection Agency (EPA), the DOE helped establish the Energy Star program, which promotes energy efficiency.

UNESCO

Goal Share scientific knowledge and promote the development of renewable energy policies

Reach Worldwide

Facts Has 981 World Heritage Sites

The United Nations Educational, Scientific and Cultural Organization (UNESCO) is an international organization. One of its goals is to help nations develop renewable energy programs to slow or halt climate change. UNESCO works toward **developing countries** having access to clean, sustainable, and affordable energy. The Renewable Energy Futures for UNESCO Sites (RENFORUS) promotes the use of UNESCO Biosphere Reserves and World Heritage Sites for renewable energy.

SE4ALL

Goal Give communities access to modern renewable energy services

Reach Worldwide

Facts Works with more than 50 developing countries

Sustainable Energy for All (SE4All) was launched by the Secretary-General of the United Nations in 2011. This group is working to transform the world's energy systems. Its goals include worldwide access to modern energy services, doubling the rate of improvement in efficient energy use, and doubling the use of renewable energy by 2030. Nearly one in five people worldwide do not have access to modern energy services.

REN 21

Goal Provide ways to help people exchange knowledge in order to increase renewable energy use around the world

Reach Worldwide

Facts Publishes an annual Renewables Global Status Report developed by more than 500 international experts

The Renewable Energy Policy Network for the 21st Century (REN 21), which was launched in 2005, brings governments, international organizations, scientists, educators, and others together to solve renewable energy issues. The network's goal is to develop polices to encourage the use of wind, water, solar, and other renewable energy sources. REN 21 allows people to track, share, and gather data on the various renewable energy initiatives around the world.

Research a Renewable Energy Issue

The Issue

Many people have different opinions about the use of renewable energy. People disagree about what types of renewable energy to use, or whether it is necessary to develop. It is important to enter into a discussion to hear all points of view before making decisions. Discussing issues will ensure that the actions taken are beneficial for all involved.

Get the Facts

Choose an issue from this book. Then, pick one of the four points of view presented in the issue spectrum. Using the book and researching in the library or on the Internet, find out more about the group you chose. What is important to members of this group? Why are they backing or opposing this particular issue? What claims or facts can they use to support their point of view? Be sure to write clear and concise supporting arguments for your group. Focus on renewable energy use and the way the group's needs relate to it. Will this group be affected in a positive or negative way by the actions offered?

Use the Concept Web

A concept web is a useful research tool. Read the information and review the structure in the concept web on the next page. Use the relationships between concepts to help you understand your group's point of view.

Organize Your Research

Sort your information into organized points. Make sure your research answers clearly what impact the issue will have on your chosen group, how that impact will affect them, and why they have chosen their specific point of view.

RENEWABLE ENERGY CONCEPT WEB

Use this concept web to understand the network of factors relating to solar energy, hydropower, wind energy, biofuels, biomass, and geothermal energy.

- Gives off little or no pollution
- Is a free fuel
- Has widespread use in areas that receive a great deal of sunlight

- Gives off no greenhouse emissions
- Accounts for about 20 percent of world's electricity
- Can damage ecosystems

- Has high construction costs
- Has low operating costs
- Gives off no pollution
- Can spoil the beauty of landscapes
- Can be unreliable source when wind does not blow

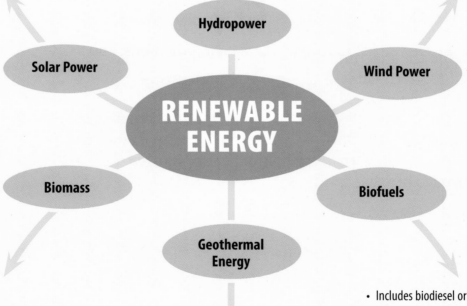

RENEWABLE ENERGY

Hydropower

Solar Power

Wind Power

Biomass

Biofuels

Geothermal Energy

- Is sustainable
- Uses organic waste materials
- Is inexpensive

- Includes biodiesel or bioalcohol fuels made from plants
- Can be expensive to produce

- Is energy from inside Earth
- Is abundant
- Gives off no pollution
- Is a reliable source of energy

Test Your Knowledge

Answer each of the questions below to test your
knowledge of the renewable energy issue.

1 What country is home
to the world's largest
hydroelectric dam?

2 What percentage
of Earth is covered
by water?

3 What is electricity
measured in?

4 Name the machine that
is a modern version of
the ancient waterwheel.

5 Wood, agricultural
crops, and cow manure
are examples of what kind
of fuel?

6 What powers
the Sun?

7 What tiny units
of light or other
electromagnetic energy do
photovoltaic cells capture?

8 Name the three types
of solar power.

9 What is biofuel
made from?

10 What renewable
energy comes from
the heat of Earth's interior?

ANSWERS 1. China **2.** More than 70 percent **3.** Watts **4.** Turbine **5.** Biomass
6. Fusion **7.** Photons **8.** Passive solar energy, solar thermal, and photovoltaic
9. Plants **10.** Geothermal

Key Words

array: a group of solar panels, containing photovoltaic cells

atoms: the smallest units of an element that have all the properties of that element

carbon dioxide: an odorless, colorless gas that is a part of Earth's atmosphere and that is produced when fossil fuels are burned

climate change: a change in average temperatures and other weather conditions over a long period of time, such as the major warming trend that most scientists agree has been taking place over the past century

developing countries: countries with low average income that until recently had little manufacturing and technology

ecosystem: a system formed by the interaction of plants and animals with the environment

efficient: working without waste of energy

electrons: tiny particles with negative electric charges that orbit the nucleus, or center, of an atom

elements: basic substances that are made of atoms of only one kind and that cannot be broken down by ordinary chemical means

emissions: gases or other substances released into the air

genes: molecular units of a living thing that pass traits to the next generation

geothermal: relating to the heat of Earth's interior

geysers: natural hot springs that send out sprays of steam and water from time to time

green: promoting or beneficial to environmentalism

helium: a very light gaseous chemical element that does not burn and is used in balloons

incentives: ways to encourage people to do something

methane: a gas with no color or smell that burns easily and is used as a fuel

organic materials: substances that are related to or obtained from living things

parabolic: shaped like the inside of a bowl

photons: tiny units of light or other electromagnetic energy with no mass or electric charge

pollution: substances that can make air, water, or land dirty or harmful

radiation: energy in rays or waves that is given off, as with the Sun

reservoir: a natural or artificial place where water is collected and stored for later use

semiconductors: materials, such as silicon, that allow some electricity to move through them

species: a group of individuals with common characteristics

subsidies: financial aid, as given by the government

sustainable: capable of being maintained without harming the environment

tectonic plates: sections of Earth's surface that move very slowly

turbines: devices that use the energy of moving water, air, or steam hitting their blades in order to rotate

wind farm: an area in which a number of wind turbines are placed in order to produce electricity

Index

Log on to www.av2books.com

AV² by Weigl brings you media enhanced books that support active learning. Go to www.av2books.com, and enter the special code found on page 2 of this book. You will gain access to enriched and enhanced content that supplements and complements this book. Content includes video, audio, weblinks, quizzes, a slide show, and activities.

AV² Online Navigation

Book Pages
AV² pages directly correspond to pages in the book.

Audio
Listen to sections of the book read aloud.

Video
Watch informative video clips.

Key Words
Study vocabulary, and complete a matching word activity.

Embedded Weblinks
Gain additional information for research.

Quizzes
Test your knowledge.

Slide Show
View images and captions, and prepare a presentation.

Try This!
Complete activities and hands-on experiments.

AV² was built to bridge the gap between print and digital. We encourage you to tell us what you like and what you want to see in the future.

Sign up to be an AV² Ambassador at www.av2books.com/ambassador.

Due to the dynamic nature of the Internet, some of the URLs and activities provided as part of AV² by Weigl may have changed or ceased to exist. AV² by Weigl accepts no responsibility for any such changes. All media enhanced books are regularly monitored to update addresses and sites in a timely manner. Contact AV² by Weigl at 1-866-649-3445 or av2books@weigl.com with any questions, comments, or feedback.

W9-ANT-374

Yoko Tanaka

DANDELION'S DREAM

Special thanks to my London crit group: Bridget Marzo, Layn Marlow, Heather Kilgour, Cliff McNish, Andrew Weale, Jane Porter, Anne-Marie Perks, Loretta Schauer, Candy Gourlay, Joseph Coelho, Charles Wilkinson, and Patrick Miller; and to Emma Lawlor and Jo Haas.

Dedicated to Dan

CANDLEWICK PRESS

Copyright © 2020 by Yoko Tanaka

All rights reserved. No part of this book may be reproduced, transmitted, or stored in an information retrieval system in any form or by any means, graphic, electronic, or mechanical, including photocopying, taping, and recording, without prior written permission from the publisher.

First edition 2020

Library of Congress Catalog Card Number pending

ISBN 978-1-5362-0453-7

CCP 24 23 22 21 20 19
10 9 8 7 6 5 4 3 2 1

Printed in Shenzhen, Guangdong, China

The illustrations for this book were done in charcoal and colored digitally.

Candlewick Press
99 Dover Street
Somerville, Massachusetts 02144

visit us at www.candlewick.com

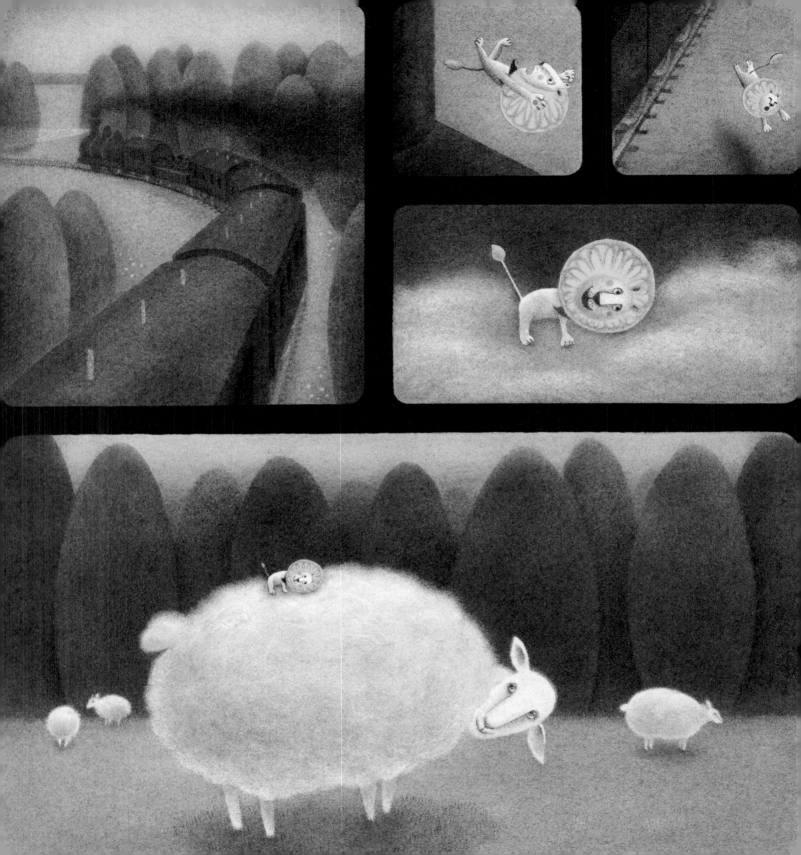

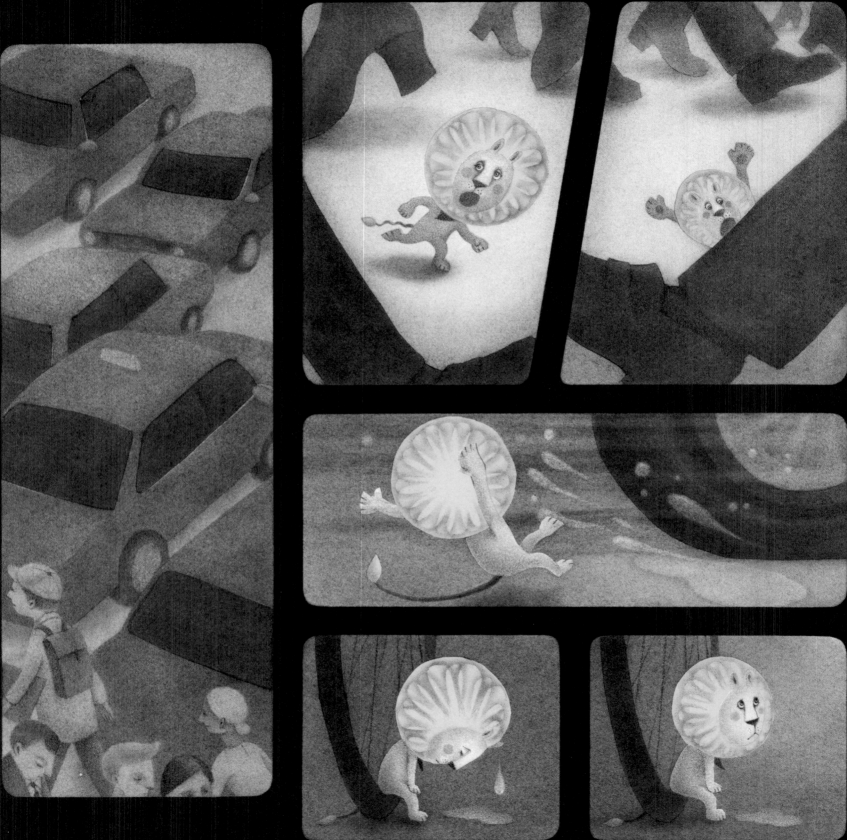

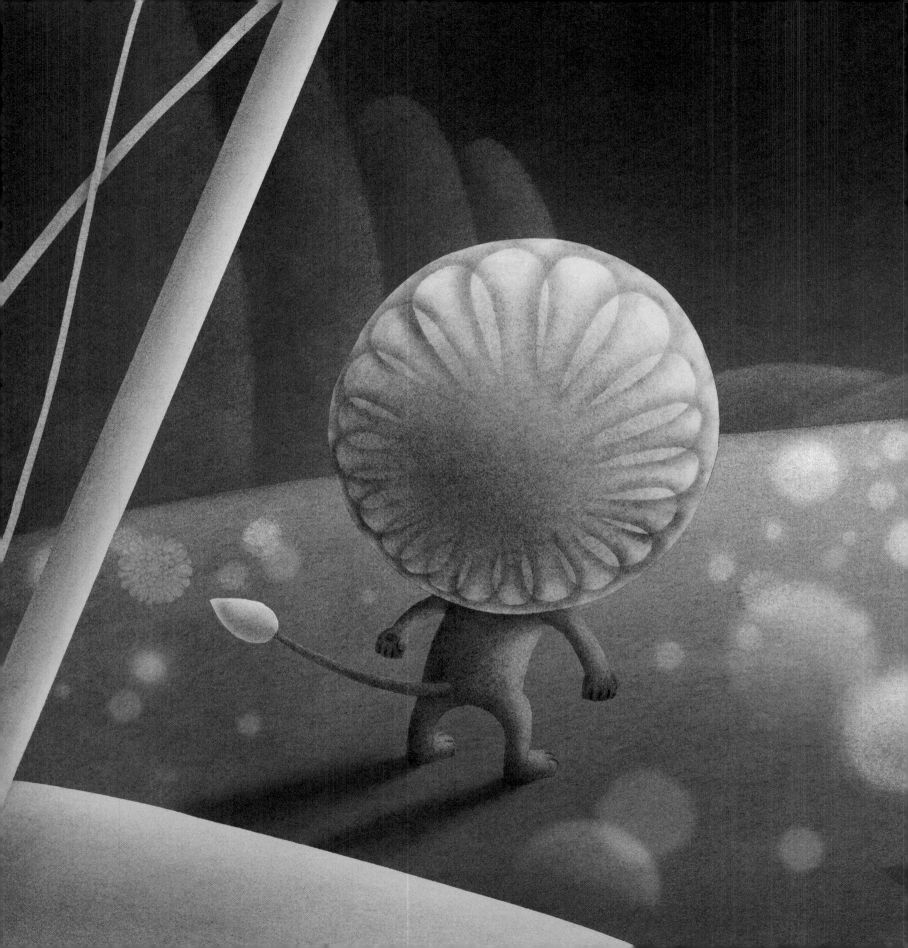

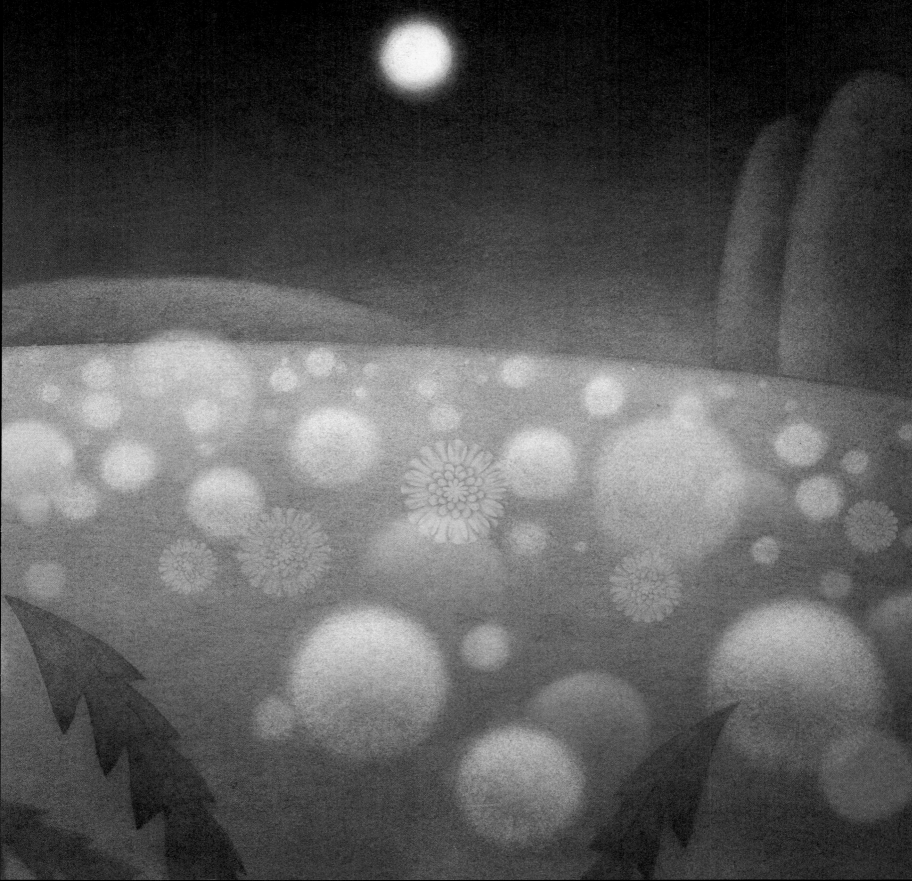

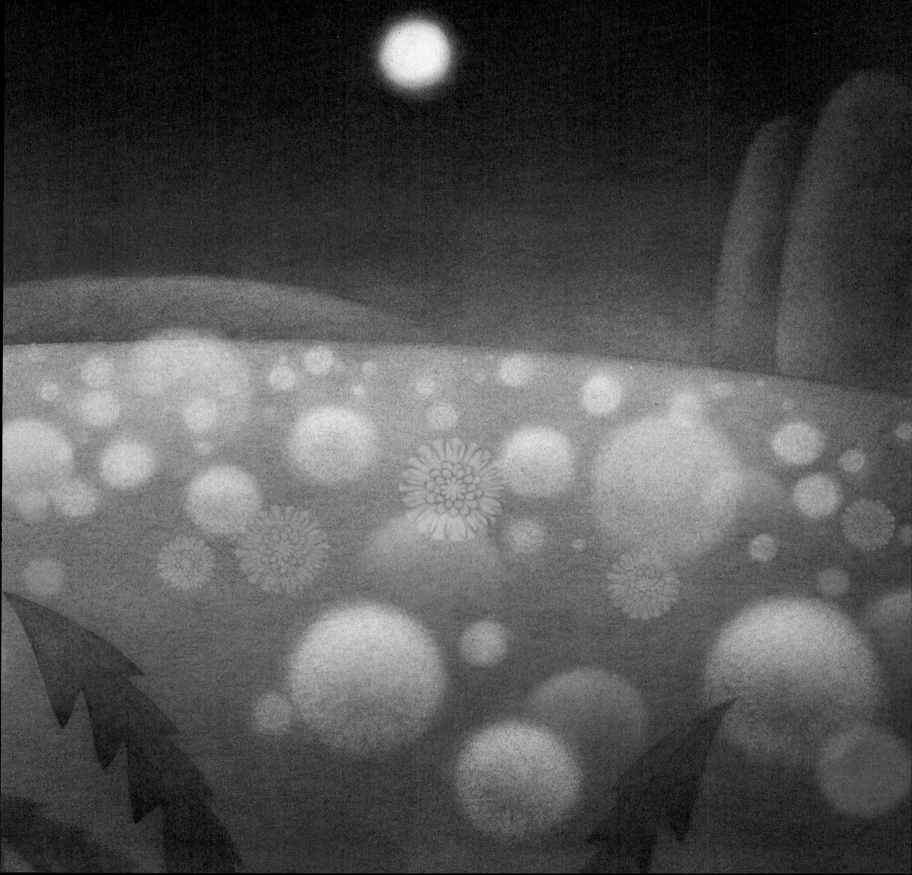

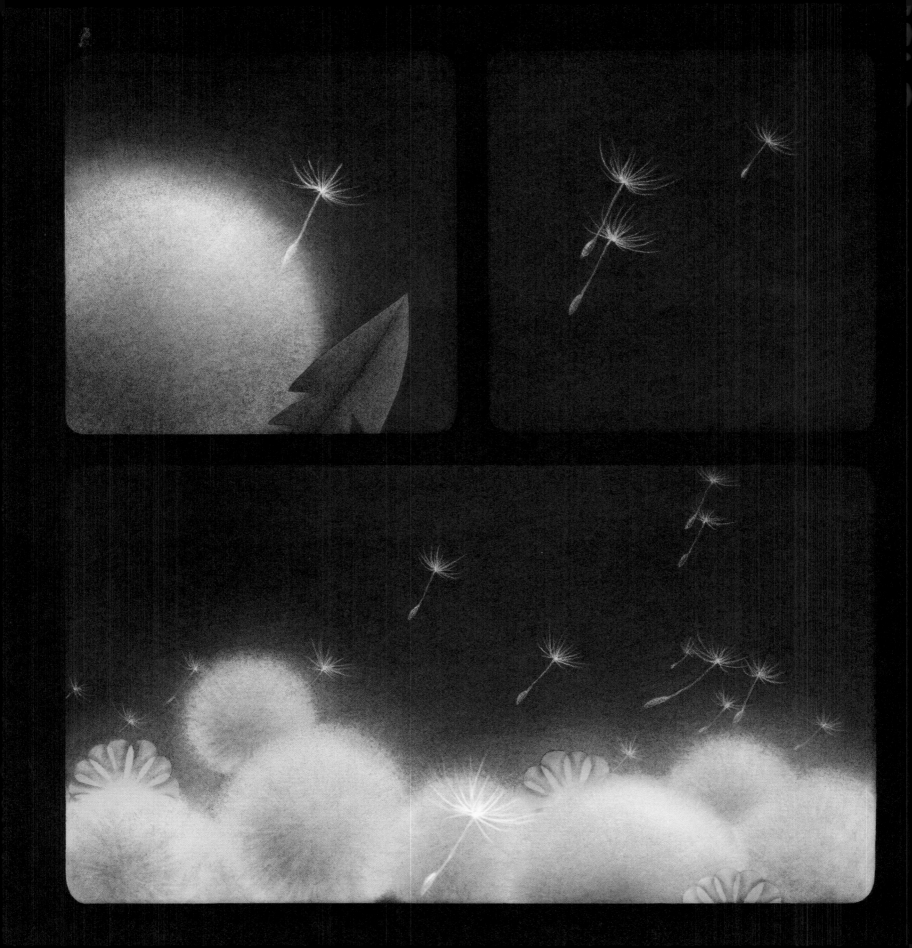